ORKNEY

Like a painting seen through the lens, a fulmar sits on its nest

ORKNEY

PHOTOGRAPHS BY
GUNNIE MOBERG

WITH AN INTRODUCTION BY
DUNCAN McLEAN

BIRLINN

First published in Great Britain in 2006 by
Birlinn Ltd
West Newington House
10 Newington Road
Edinburgh EH9 1QS

www.birlinn.co.uk

ISBN10: 1 84158 445 2
ISBN13: 978 1 84158 445 4

British Library Cataloguing-in-Publication Data
A catalogue record for this book is available on request from the British Library

Printed in Malta for compass Press Ltd

PREFACE

I have been living and photographing in Orkney now for thirty years and the landscape never fails to inspire me. The days never seem the same; all the islands have their own characteristics, some green and low-lying with good agricultural land, others brown with peat and heather. The beautiful coastline of Orkney changes from soaring cliffs full of birdlife to sandy beaches and rocky shores where sheep live entirely on sea-weed.

I started off very much a media photographer, by chance really as there were few photographers working in Orkney when I moved there. I covered many news stories for the local and national newspapers. It was an exciting time – I was always rushing to the airport with films, not knowing if what I had was what was wanted until I saw the papers the next day, and not knowing if I had made the front page or not. It was all a bit nerve-racking. The various picture editors were relying on you and you *had* to do a good job to get more work coming your way.

When I first arrived I was very fortunate to meet Captain Andy Alsop and his wife, Glenys. Andy was then head of Loganair, the local airline, and asked me if I wanted to come flying with him. I think that changed my life more than anything else. Seeing Orkney from the air was just amazing. For years I did a lot of aerial photography. I loved the patterns of silage cutting in the summer, the many archaeological sites, looking like pieces of jewellery far below me, and the low light in winter, which showed up the texture of the landscape and made wonderful long shadows along the dykes and ditches.

As well as my news work and landscape photography, there have been many other things going on in Orkney too. The St Magnus Festival, a feast of music, drama and poetry which brings celebrities from all over the world, started in 1977, and I was to photograph events and performances for the next twenty years. It was a lucrative and enjoyable time, having all these famous people on my doorstep, so to speak.

Our two local celebrities, George Mackay Brown and Peter Maxwell Davies, were always in demand by newspapers and magazines. Over the years I was to illustrate many books by George, and in the last one we did together, before he died in 1996, the roles were reversed – George was writing poems for my pictures. Sadly, he never saw the book finished.

I have also worked on many books with my Norwegian friend, historian Liv Schei. We have travelled to every corner of Orkney, Shetland and the Faroe Islands. It has been a fascinating experience to illustrate her books as I have taken pictures that I normally would not have taken, and of course during our travels I met a lot of wonderful people.

I exhibit regularly, which gives me a chance to show my more personal pictures, and a more abstract side of the Orkney landscape. It is also nice to see a whole body of one's work together, in a gallery.

When asked to do this book for Birlinn, I felt a bit at a loss. Without any running text to accompany the pictures, where would I begin? However, once I learnt that Duncan McLean had agreed to write the introduction, and once I started to assemble pictures, it became easier. I have included pictures of places I feel people should not miss on a visit to Orkney, as well as others which I feel are just lovely places to see, if time permits.

Whether this book is bought as a souvenir to take home after a visit to Orkney, or is bought by Orcadians for themselves or as a gift for friends or family who live elsewhere, I hope it contains something for everyone to enjoy.

Gunnie Moberg, January 2006

Ring of Brogar, henge monument, 3rd millennium BC. The moon rises over the circle of twenty-seven standing stones. It is likely that there were originally sixty stones.

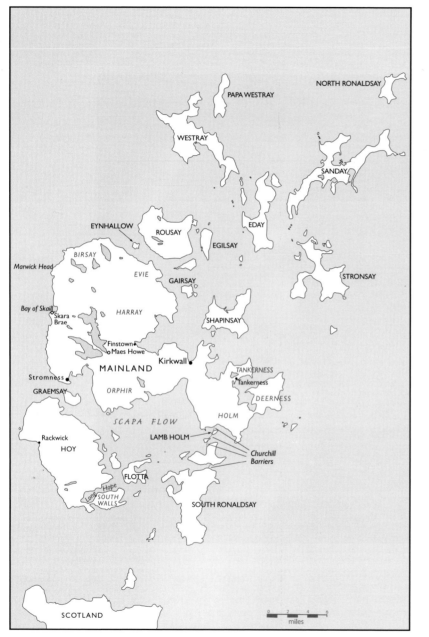

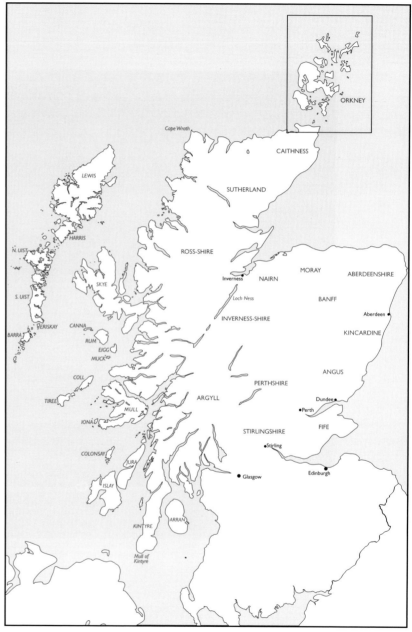

INTRODUCTION

Our house is a small one. But it sits on a low, south-facing hill, with a quiet single-track road leading down through fields to the shore. With the house door open on a calm summer's day, the road feels like an extension of the back lobby, and instead of sitting at the kitchen table, we often find ourselves down amongst the rocks and birds of the Coldomo shore.

The rocks in this part of Orkney split easily into flagstones, and all along the shore here weathering has chiseled apart the layers of slabs, dragged them up and down, left and right, and piled them on top of each other. Sandstone armchairs and tabletops are scattered about the place like a Neolithic furniture warehouse. I like to sit back in one of these chairs, put my feet up on the barnacled coffee table in front of me, and gradually sink back into the landscape, into invisibility.

For the first thing you notice as you walk down onto the Coldomo shore is that, if this is a domestic space, it's not really your own. It may feel like an extension of your kitchen, but for the birds it really is a kitchen, dining room and bedroom combined. The last few yards of the track are hidden by the willows along the old millburn, so when you step down onto the sand it's like you're bursting from nowhere into the birds' private space. Dozens of shalders go peeping off across the sand. The various gulls seem to be a bit more complacent, and tend to just stand up straighter, cast a cold yellow eye over you, and give a few skraiks of warning to each other – or to me. Redshanks and sandpipers take to the wing, their alarm cries echoing the local name for them: Water Pleeps. So within ten seconds of stepping out of the willows, the shore and the air are full of flapping, scowling, screeling birds, put off their supper-hunt, sleep disturbed, mating rituals cruelly interrupted.

I feel like a housebreaker. So I walk quickly for half a minute, fording the millburn's outfall at the stepping-stones, and find a slabby armchair to recline in, to disappear into. Happily, disappearance seems easy to achieve. Once I'm sitting at peace, the birds are tolerant of my intrusion, and after a minute's passed have settled back into whatever they were doing before I broke and entered.

This isn't one of Orkney's most beautiful or dramatic shores. One of the advantages of that is that very few folk ever bother to come here, apart from those like myself who actually live within a few hundred yards of it. Sightseers and tourists don't seek this place out the way they do the spectacular cliffs and rockstacks at Yesnaby, or the colossal boulders of Rackwick Bay. One of the benefits of this neglect is that, although an intruder like myself might ruffle a few feathers once or twice a day, the birds aren't constantly disturbed by visitors stomping through their home; there's not nearly enough nuisance to persuade them to flit off somewhere quieter.

No, the rare human visitor is accepted, or at least tolerated; just as, I suppose, the occasional gale or freak wave must be tholed. So much the better for me, and the few others who make it down to spots like this (and Gunnie Moberg is undoubtedly one of us.) If we sit back and watch, or walk slowly and quietly wherever we're going, then nature parts before us and closes up behind us more or less seamlessly.

Walking southwards from here, the sea on my right hand, I pass the farm of Coldomo. One day a couple of summers ago, I was sitting on a rock just the other side of the millburn when a sound of many scuttering feet made me look this way. And there was a sight I'd never seen before: the Coldomo farmer and three of his dogs driving a large flock of sheep along the beach. It was almost surreal. You're so used to seeing sheep wandering green grassy fields that it seemed barely believable to see them picking their way past rockpools, lurching quickly forwards across the sandy stretches, some of them even stopping occasionally to have a nibble at a strand of kelp or a patch of seapinks. And the sheepdogs, as well as hugging the sand with their bellies behind the flock, would dart out occasionally into the lapping surf, splashing through the shallows, using threats and menaces to keep the sheep on the straight and narrow strand. After ten minutes or so, the dogs turned the sheep up the track to the mill, and so on, to some fresh field or pasture new.

I don't suppose beaches are used every day, even in Orkney, for moving livestock from one grazing to another. But occasionally, as on that day below Coldomo, it makes all the sense necessary. It reminds you that features of the landscape we tend to think of as existing in themselves, rather than leading anywhere — features we might even think of as obstacles — have often in the past been perceived quite differently. The sea itself is the most obvious example. We usually think of it as a difficult and dangerous part of the world, a place that insanely courageous individuals venture into after white fish or the black, black oil. Or at best it's something that we cross with some trepidation and plenty of seasick tablets on the ro-ro ferry. But until little more than a century ago many parts of Orkney — and most of wilder landscapes in Shetland and the west Highlands — had very little in the way of roads or even decent tracks. A twenty-minute row across a bay or sea-loch could be a swift alternative to a three-hour walk on the sheeptrack round the head of the voe.

So it is, I suppose, that the stretch of water between this shore and the town of Stromness three or so miles away is known as the Cairston Roads. Thousands of vessels — from Viking longships and the great herring fleets of the past, to the passenger ferries and the wreck-diving charter boats of today — have plied that stretch of water seemingly as casually as if it were a smooth tarmacadamed road.

Of course on a road you don't get Solan Geese plunging into the water around you, nor porpoises shadowing your car as you drive along, nor whiskered seals watching curiously from the skerries as you pass.

I recently asked Gunnie if there was a theme or a word or an image that summed up Orkney for her. She didn't have to think long before replying 'stone.' One of her early books, full of starkly beautiful black-and-white photos, was called *Stone*. And the textures, colours and shapes of stone continue to fascinate her: from the massive standing stones she manages to make look delicate and sky-bound, to the ridged furrow-like shore rocks of Warebeth catching the low winter sunshine, to the miles of dykes and the hundreds of sheep pounds and tangle steethes that throw their stony web across the landscape.

If someone asked me the same question, I might be tempted to answer 'work.' For holidaymakers, their time in Orkney is by definition about not working. But for those who live here – natives and resident aliens, such as myself – work tends to fill in the days pretty thoroughly. We don't get a lot of time to gaze at the stunning hillscape of Hoy, or to watch the way the wind shakes the barley, or the poppies nod by the roadside. Until very recently – sixty years ago for the more accessible parts of Orkney, just a few years for some of the remoter islands – we were living in what was largely a subsistence economy. Sure, there was a mixture of feudalism on some of the big island estates and capitalism in the shops and marts of the two market towns. But the majority of folk were small farmers, who grew crops for their own consumption – tatties for food, barley for beer – and raised a cow or two for milk, butter and cheese. Surplus crops were sold or traded, and of course ambitious farmers could raise extra cattle or sheep to sell for slaughter at the right time of the year. But most Orcadians' efforts most of the time were dedicated to piecing together their own sustenance.

We're past that stage now, and most people think that's a positive development (though some of the smaller outer isles, struggling to find any other economic activity that can sustain them, might argue that subsistence farming had its good points.) But still it's a struggle to carve out a living in a small community, with a limited population to buy your wares or services. It takes enterprise, effort and imagination to thrive. Gunnie's portraits rarely feature Orcadians taking their ease in an idyllic island environment. Far more often they're busy being enterprising or imaginative: collecting spoots, feeding their rare-breed pigs, or selling their pounds of good steak mince.

Just beyond Coldomo, there's a place where a natural break in the rocks of the shore has been widened into a channel about eight feet across and three feet deep. You see these artificial cuttings at various points around Orkney, but I have to admit I've no idea who created them or when. They obviously date to a period when the farmers who lived inland also ran out small fishing boats on a pretty regular basis. But that only narrows down the timescale to: somewhere between 2000 BC and the Beatles' first LP.

Whenever the job was done, it must have been incredibly hard, back-braking work, breaking rocks in the hot sun and the cold, kelpy sea. Yet crucial enough for the safety of the yole and its crew, and for the success of the fishing, to invest months or years of labour in. What else can you do? If your farm has a rocky foreshore, you have to cut a path through the rocks – or risk wreck or starvation.

As chance would have it, it's at this point that the harbour of Stromness becomes visible, as I've walked far enough to see past Bu Point. I say 'visible', but really I should say 'audible', as at the moment there's a constant thumping din as an extended pier is piled-in for the new, super-ferry between here and the Scottish mainland.

It's impossible not to compare the two constructions. The small group of men painstakingly chipping away at the bedrock over countless low-tide summer days, their hands blistering as they swung the malls and wielded the crowbars. And the high-tech team of sat-nav-positioned piledrivers and giant cranes, the concrete pourers and the dumper trucks. . . and the teams of men with their malls and shovels and blistered hands.

It would be easy to get sentimental about the noble efforts of our ancestors as they struggled with nature and geology to clear a way to their living. But I suppose today's town planners and surveyors and labourers are engaged in exactly the same struggle: using every tool at their disposal to shape nature to their economic ends. These days the tools are bigger and louder, and the ends are different too: nationwide commerce and the tourist industry, rather than local trade and inshore fishing. But it's all about making a living, by any means necessary.

Come to think of it, the story of human beings along the Orkney shore is really not much more than that. And the relationship between us and 'nature' has never been much different either – neither more nor less. We've been happy to sit on the rocks to fish for cuithes, or to hack through them to make safe passage for our creel boats. We've gathered the kelp and tangles off the shore after high seas, and spread it on the fields for fertilizer, or rendered it down to alginates to sell to glass and soap manufacturers. We've gathered gulls' eggs off the cliffs, and we've swauped for auks – as the Faroese still do – catching guillemots for their meat. We've even provided shelter and support to vast navies of fighting boats in two world wars and beyond.

These days we're more in favour of wreck charters and cruise liners, lobster creelers and scallop divers, even vast island-sized tankers that slip in at the southern entrance to Scapa Flow and drink in millions of gallons of oil before heading off to refineries in Hull or Rotterdam. But it's just the latest chapter in the same old story, the tale of to and fro between the people and the place, between human nature and nature wild.

And that, by the way, is where you find Gunnie time and again in these photographs: in between the human and the natural. There's a lot of landscape here, but it's landscape shaped and patterned by thousands of years of concerted human effort. And on the other hand, when she takes you close to the people of Orkney, we're often toiling away in the midst of beauty that would take the breath away if familiarity hadn't made us so blind to it. That's the place that Gunnie takes us to again and again. It's a very Orcadian place. It's a good place to be.

Duncan McLean
January 2006

Brough of Birsay, tidal island, Mainland, 8th-12th century AD. Prior to the arrival of the Norsemen, there was a thriving Pictish community on the island. Centuries of history to look at and puffins too!

Scrimshaw on sperm whale teeth, by a Birsay whaler

Melsetter House, Longhope, Hoy, AD 1898. Apart from Rysa Lodge, also on Hoy, Melsetter House is William R. Lethaby's sole work in Scotland and the most beautiful country house in Orkney, inside and out.

The garden at Kirbister Farm Museum, Birsay, Mainland. Built in 1723 and restored in 1987.

The interior of the 'firehouse', formerly the kitchen or 'but' end, at Kirbister Farm Museum

The East Mainland Agricultural Show, Deerness. August is the month for the shows, bringing people and animals together from all over Orkney.

The Stones of Stenness, early 3rd millennium BC. Only four stones of the circle now survive, the tallest being over 5m high. It is likely that there were originally twelve stones, set in a circle.

Stromness Shopping Week, a yearly event of fun for young and old, visitors too

Fancy Dress Walkers: 'Mardi Gras'

Fancy Dress Walkers: 'Homer and Marge Simpson'

For four days children produced drawings inspired by the circus coming to town. Organised and put up by the Pier Arts Centre, Stromness, it made a colourful display.

The Earl's Palace, Kirkwall, AD 1606. This splendid building, with a magnificent hall, has been described as 'possibly the most mature and accomplished piece of Renaissance architecture left in Scotland'.

Digging for 'spoots' or razorfish at low spring tide in Stromness. A meal loved by many locals.

Eynhallow Church, Eynhallow, 12th century AD. The name Eynhallow means 'Holy Isle' from Old Norse 'Eyin Helga', which suggests that there may have been a small Celtic monastery here.

Orphir, West Mainland. A lovely spread in summer is the vivid red patches of colour that the poppies make along the roadside and along dykes.

Stone of Setter, Eday, 2nd millennium BC. Furrowed by weathering, this monolith is 4.5m high and stands in a dominating position overlooking several chambered tombs.

The North Ronaldsay seaweed-eating sheep live outside the 13-mile stone dyke which surrounds the island and are only let in at lambing time

When the clipping and dipping seasons arrive in North Ronaldsay, the sheep are herded off the beaches into stone-built 'punds'

Mine Howe, Tankerness, East Mainland, the newest opened mound in Orkney. The mystery of the 29 steps down into darkness is still to be solved. A symbolic entry into the underworld?

Coming up the steep and very narrow steps at Mine Howe. It helps being young!

The Bay of Skaill, West Mainland. Interesting rock formations can be seen all along the coast from Stromness to Birsay. A good walk for visitors interested in geology.

St Magnus Church, Egilsay, 12th century AD, dedicated to Magnus Erlendsson, the Earl who was murdered on the island *c.*1117. Although roofless, the church is otherwise virtually complete, and its elegant tower still dominates the island.

Sowing oats by hand was done until 2004 at Antabreck, North Ronaldsay

Being greeted by a beautiful horse; a Highland pony at South Ness, North Ronaldsay

Mosses and grasses, a disarray of colours on the way to Muckle Water, Rousay. The loch is good for trout fishing.

In late summer the cotton grass, *Eriophorum sp.*, seen here from the old Finstown road, Mainland, makes you stop to admire its beauty

The impressive sand dunes at Tresness, Sanday. At low tide, the beach seems to go on for miles.

Early days: The Wrigley Sisters at their 'Centre of Muisc' in Kirkwall. Now world renowned, they still take time out to promote music locally.

The massive boulder of gneiss at Scar, Sanday, weighing over 20 tonnes and transported from Norway by ice

Waulkmill Bay, Orphir, Mainland. A beautiful sheltered sandy beach when the tide is out; and when the tide comes in, a warm place for a swim.

Click Mill, Dounby, Mainland. The only surviving example of a horizontal watermill in Orkney. Built around 1823, it has been restored and all the machinery is in working order.

Interior of the Dounby watermill. These horizontal mills have been known since Norse times.

The lovely plantation of mixed trees at Binscarth, near Finstown, Mainland. Planted in the 19th century, it is one of the few areas of woodland in Orkney.

Early Autumn evening, looking west towards the Bay of Skaill and Skaill House, West Mainland

Orkney 'Make Poverty History' marchers, crossing the bridge over the two lochs, Harray and Stenness, prior to the G8 summit at Gleneagles in 2005

Pool of Cletts, East Mainland, with St Peter's Church in the distance. George Low was strongly moved by its beauty during his wanderings in South Ronaldsay in the 18th century.

Looking over Kirkwall from Sunnybank Road

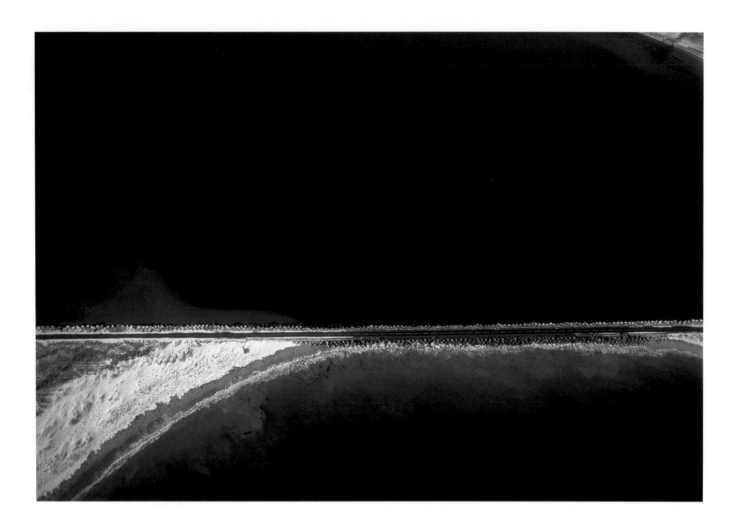

Churchill Barrier No. 4. Italian prisoners of war arrived in 1942 to help with the building of the four barriers.

The Italian Chapel, Lamb Holm. At their camp, the Italian POWs turned two Nissen Huts into a chapel, now one of the most visited sites in Orkney.

Interior of the Italian Chapel, Lamb Holm. Domenico Chiochetti was one of the driving forces in creating the chapel. He returned to Orkney twice to restore the paintwork.

An unusual picture of a grey (Atlantic) seal pup. Born on land, a 'white coat' is never seen in the water, but this pool must have been too tempting.

After 3–4 weeks of suckling its mother's rich milk and shedding its white coat, this pup is ready to face the stormy winter seas

Mountains of golden barley at the Highland Park Distillery, Kirkwall. Founded in 1798 it is still going strong. Their unique 12-year-old single malt is known worldwide.

Three well-known contributors to the Orkney arts scene

Writer George Mackay Brown

Composer Peter Maxwell Davies

Film maker Margaret Tait

In the Western Ocean is Suleskerry, one of the biggest puffin colonies in Britain, which is home to some 44,000 pairs

Young shags, Suleskerry. Shags are numerous in Orkney and can be seen along the coastlines and on skerries.

Kittiwakes at Marwick Head, West Mainland. A wonderful place for watching various birds in their thousands.

Primula Scotia. This little flower is special to northern Scotland and can be seen in Papa Westray and a few other places in Orkney.

St Michael's Kirk, Harray, Mainland. Built in 1836, its hilltop vantage point overlooks the whole parish of Harray.

The well-known writer Eric Linklater is buried in Harray Churchyard, his wife Marjorie beside him. Their stones overlook their home, Merkister, now a hotel.

Rusk Holm, off Westray. This 'fort' was built on the rocks for the sheep. In bad weather, they could get cut off from the holm and drown.

Coming down to the Bay of Skaill, West Mainland, passing St Peter's Church (1836), a fine building of its period

Skara Brae, Skaill, West Mainland. This Stone Age village emerged during a storm in the middle of the 19th century and is the biggest tourist attraction in Orkney.

Quoyloo Church, West Mainland (19th century), the most vividly decorated Presbyterian church in Orkney. The colour scheme was proposed by Orkney artist Stanley Cursiter, His Majesty's Limner in Scotland.

St Margaret's Hope, South Ronaldsay. A winter scene of the village. Snow seldom lies more than a few days.

At Little Noup Head, Eday, an interesting outcrop of Upper Eday Sandstone emerges out of the sea   Looking down at a section of Upper Eday Sandstone

A bored unicorn

Goat with lovely lugs

Decorated from top to bottom

On show at the Dounby Agricultural show, a Cambell Oil Engine from 1904

Yesnaby, West Mainland, with a sprinkling of snow. A beautiful, unspoilt area with a spectacular coastline.

Hoy Sound at low tide, from the Noust of Nethertoun, Stromness

Graham Place, Stromness, early Sunday morning

The strong heaving, white-foaming tidal race between Evie and the island of Eynhallow

Sandfiold Tomb, West Mainland, 2000 BC. A unique flagstone cist was found in 1989, containing three burials. One was a large urn with cremated remains. Cists were always used for single burials.

The 13-mile long road around the island of Rousay has wonderful views over the Orkney Mainland and the isles

A piece of carved Portland stone, weighing just under 15 tonnes, was transported to Rousay in 2005. The sculpture is the work of poet Ian Hamilton Finlay.

Midhowe Broch, Rousay, *c.* 2nd century BC – *c.* 2nd century AD. The stretch from Westness, along the shore to Midhowe broch, is described as the most important archaeological mile in Scotland.

Glowing in the winter light, the road to Yesnaby, West Mainland

The Broch of Gurness, Evie, 2nd century BC. Gurness has the most extensive and well-preserved domestic buildings surrounding the broch to be seen anywhere in Scotland.

Noup Head, Westray, one of the largest seabird colonies in Britain. In May and June, the cliffs are alive with birds – kittiwakes, guillemots and razorbills.

Balfour Castle, Shapinsay, mid 19th century but built around an older existing house. The Scottish Baronial style castle has a fine drawing room and conservatory.

Hall of Rendall Dovecote, West Mainland, 17th century. This attractive dovecote has four external string-courses and is unique in the Northern Isles.

The pigeons' nest in irregular gaps left in the masonry in the internal wall-face

The Loons, Birsay, West Mainland. Birdwatching from the RSPB hide is very rewarding. Waders and ducks appear from the reeds and other birds will fly in for a bath.

Greylag geese make a stop-over at the Loch of Banks, Birsay, West Mainland, on their way south in October

Langskaill House, Gairsay, 17th century. The *Orkneyinga Saga* tells us the Viking Svein Asleifarson farmed on the island and remains of his great hall are believed to lie beneath the present house.

Marwick, West Mainland, a lovely area of green and fertile fields. Cattle graze in lush grass and among wildflowers.

Moncur Memorial Church, Stronsay. Designed by Leslie Graham MacDougall and built in 1955, the building is curiously old fashioned and its cruciform design is decidedly un-Presbyterian in form.

Whitehall Village, Stronsay. By the early 20th century, the village had become one of the most important places in Europe to land and salt herring for export.

The Ring of Brogar, Mainland, 3rd millennium BC. The Ness of Brogar was a perfect place to choose for a great ceremonial monument, being set firmly in the fertile heart of Orkney.

Holm of Huip, Stronsay, an important breeding site for Atlantic Grey Seals who have their pups in October/November

Hoy dominates much of the Orkney landscape, with its two peaks, Cuilags and Ward Hill

The huge bay of Rackwick, on the west side of Hoy, with its beautiful long, sandy beach

The Dwarfie Stane, a rock-cut tomb, Hoy, 3rd millennium BC. Hollowing out this tomb with stone tools must have been a horrendous task. The boulder outside is the original blocking stone.

The red and yellow sandstone cliffs on the west side of Hoy have been eroded by the sea into spectacular verticals and seastacks

A winter screen of the south end of Hoy, looking across The Ayre to South Walls

Lyness Naval Cemetery, Hoy. Here rest the heroes from two world wars – from the battle of Jutland, 1916, to HMS *Royal Oak*, torpedoed in Scapa Flow, 1939, with the loss of 833 men.

The soaring cliffs of the west side Hoy and the 450-ft sea stack, the Old Man of Hoy, Orkney's most famous landmark

Diving on the scuttled German fleet in Scapa Flow, or on the block ships in more shallow waters, is a big tourist attraction in Orkney

Peat is still being cut in Orkney. Although most people use coal, oil and electricity, an open peat fire is still something special

Fish drying in the wind, A rare sight these days, but a lot of older people still enjoy a traditional meal

Sandside, with Hoy High Lighthouse. Graemsay is an island completely unspoilt, seldom visited by tourists, yet easily accessible from Stromness.

Deerness, South Mainland, has lovely sandy beaches like this one at Dingieshowe, and further to the east, at Newark Bay

St Magnus Cathedral, Kirkwall, 12th–15th centuries AD. In the centre of town, the magnificent, red sandstone cathedral glows in the evening light.

The west side of Hoy, with the 'Old Man'. In a different light, the red sandstone cliffs become a dark silhouette against the sky.

St Magnus Festival, in June, brings a soirée of music, poety and drama.

Festival goers, outside the cathedral   Performance inside the cathedral   Midsummer night music at the Italian Chapel, Lamb Holm

Eminent poets have performed at the St Magnus Festival over the years. Stewart Conn (right) is seen here with George MacKay Brown in 1988.

Fire practice takes place on a weekly basis at the Oil Terminal, Flotta, to make sure all personnel understand the procedures which must be undertaken in the event of an emergency

The Flotta flare can be seen from many places around Orkney

Bay of Skaill, West Mainland, looking south to the Hole O'Row, through which the sea breaks during a westerly gale

Earl's Palace, Birsay, West Mainland, 16th century AD. Built by Robert Stewart, Earl of Orkney, the striking but gaunt shell of the palace dominates the village.

Marwick Bay, West Mainland. On the headland stands the Kitchener Memorial, commemorating the loss of HMS *Hampshire* during the First World War.

Maes Howe, chambered cairn, West Mainland, early 3rd millennium BC. The tomb is considered to be one of the supreme achievements of prehistoric Europe.

Tankerness House, Kirkwall, 16th–17th century AD. One of the finest early town houses surviving in Scotland, it is now a museum.

Family of swans on Loch Stenness, West Mainland

Olive and Dora, two Gloucester Old Spot gilts, Craiglands, Birsay, West Mainland

Cock and hens at Craiglands, Birsay, West Mainland

Loch Stenness in the winter attracts hundreds of long-tailed ducks, goldeneyes and swans

Stenness, West Mainland. Orkney cattle always come to say hello!

Duncan Geddes shows off his lobsters at Orkney Seafayre in Finstown, Mainland. They sell live cockles, mussels, crabs, diver-caught scallops and farmed oysters.

Young entrepreneurs, David and Rachel Cromerty, in their new delicatessen, The Peppermill, in the centre of Kirkwall

The sheltered harbour of Stromness. The stone-built houses on the waterfront have their own piers or slipways.

Breck of Rendall, West Mainland, 19th century. Sorting sheep outside the impressive stone-built farm steading with its row of arched sheds.

Silage cutting makes the landscape turn to every shade of green during the summer months

The festival of the Horse, South Ronaldsay. After many hours of dressing, these 'horses', together with many others, are ready to join the ploughmen.

The Boys' Ploughing Match, South Ronaldsay. Having paraded with the horses, the young ploughmen proceed to the Sand O'Right, to show off their skill.

The Pier Arts Centre, Stromness, has a permanent collection of works from the St Ives School and hosts travelling and local exhibitions

Being built into the hill of Brintere's Brae, Stromness has many lanes and closes running down to the sea

The Crockness Martello Tower, Hoy, was built in 1813 to protect the entrance to Longhope against attack by American and French privateers during the Napoleonic Wars.

Kirkwall, ready for the 'Ba', a game played since 1850. Every shop and house in the centre is boarded up to take the pressure off the playing crowd.

The Christmas and New Year's Day 'Ba'' is contested in the streets with an oval form of football by two rival sides, the 'Uppies' and the 'Doonies'